# discover**more**
## *World Religions*

# What Is Christianity?

*Ernest Brazzos*

Britannica®
Educational Publishing

IN ASSOCIATION WITH

THE ROSEN
PUBLISHING
GROUP

Published in 2026 by Britannica Educational Publishing (a trademark of Encyclopædia Britannica, Inc.) in association with The Rosen Publishing Group, Inc.
2544 Clinton Street, Buffalo, NY 14224

Distributed exclusively by Rosen Publishing.
To see additional Britannica Educational Publishing titles, go to rosenpublishing.com.

Editor: Greg Roza
Book Design: Michael Flynn

Photo Credits: Cover Romolo Tavani/Shutterstock.com; (series background) Dai Yim/Shutterstock.com; p. 4 Freedom Studio/Shutterstock.com; p. 5 Porstocker/Shutterstock.com; p. 7 (top) godongphoto/Shutterstock.com; p. 7 (bottom) PeopleImages.com - Yuri A/Shutterstock.com; p. 8 WorldStockStudio/Shutterstock.com; p. 9 https://commons.wikimedia.org/wiki/File:Bautismo_de_Cristo_por_Navarrete_el_Mudo.jpg; p. 11 (top) chayanuphol/Shutterstock.com; p. 11 (bottom) Gorodenkoff/Shutterstock.com; p. 12 Shutterstock AI Generator/Shutterstock.com; p. 13 JekLi/Shutterstock.com; p. 15 (top) Renata Sedmakova/Shutterstock.com; p. 15 (bottom) PeopleImages.com - Yuri A/Shutterstock.com; p. 16 joshimerbin/Shutterstock.com; p. 17 Cineberg/Shutterstock.com; p. 19 (top) salajean/Shutterstock.com; p. 19 (bottom) https://commons.wikimedia.org/wiki/File:1099_Ascalon.jpg; p. 20 https://commons.wikimedia.org/wiki/File:Lucas_Cranach_d.%C3%84._-_Martin_Luther,_1528_(Veste_Coburg).jpg; p. 21 Morphart Creation/Shutterstock.com; p. 22 Morphart Creation/Shutterstock.com; p. 23 CL-Medien/Shutterstock.com; p. 24 Larysa Vasylenko/Shutterstock.com; p. 25 OSCAR GONZALEZ FUENTES/Shutterstock.com; p. 26 vetre / Shutterstock.com; p. 27 Africa Studio/Shutterstock.com; p. 28 Fabrizio Maffei/Shutterstock.com; p. 29 https://commons.wikimedia.org/wiki/File:Lakewood_worship.jpg.

**Cataloging-in-Publication Data**

Names: Brazzos, Ernest.
Title: What is Christianity? / Ernest Brazzos.
Description: New York : Britannica Educational Publishing, in association with Rosen Educational Services, 2026. | Series: Discover more: world religions | Includes glossary and index.
Identifiers: ISBN 9781641904582 (library bound) | ISBN 9781641904575 (pbk) | ISBN 9781641904599 (ebook)
Subjects: LCSH: Christianity--Juvenile literature.
Classification: LCC BR125.5 B74 2026 | DDC 230--dc23

Manufactured in the United States of America

Some of the images in this book illustrate individuals who are models. The depictions do not imply actual situations or events.

CPSIA Compliance Information: Batch #CSBRIT26. For further information contact Rosen Publishing at 1-800-237-9932.

Find us on

# Contents

# Christians Around the World

Christianity is the most widespread religion in the world. Nearly 2.2 billion people in the world are Christians. Like Islam and Judaism, Christianity is **monotheistic**. It teaches that there is only one God and that God created the world.

Jesus Christ is known to Christians by other names. He is "the Massiah" (savior), "Son of God," and the "Lamb of God."

Christianity also tells people to love one another and to be forgiving, humble, and kind.

Christianity is based on the life, death, and teachings of Jesus of Nazareth, who lived long ago in the Middle East. Christians believe that Jesus is the Christ, or chosen one, whom God sent to the world to save humanity. Central to Christianity is love for God above all things. Christianity has three main branches—Roman Catholicism, Eastern Orthodoxy, and Protestantism. However, Christians often see themselves as one unified community.

## WORD WISE

A MONOTHEISTIC RELIGION TEACHES THAT THERE IS ONLY ONE GOD. A POLYTHEISTIC RELIGION, ON THE OTHER HAND, TEACHES THAT THERE IS MORE THAN ONE GOD.

# Practices and Beliefs

Christians believe that Jesus was sent to Earth to suffer, die, and be resurrected to make up for people's sins. Christians view Jesus's new life after death as hope that they, too, may be granted everlasting life. Christians also believe in the Trinity. The Trinity, which means the three, is the idea that three figures are united in one God: God the Father, God the Son (Jesus), and God the Holy Spirit. The Holy Spirit is thought of as a helper sent to guide and teach people.

Christians gather together to worship in churches. Sunday is the most common day of worship. In church, Christians pray, sing, and listen to Bible readings and a sermon—a talk given by a priest or a minister.

This stained glass window depicts the Father, the Son, and the Holy Spirit (the dove).

**compareandcontrast**

What do the three figures of the Trinity have in common? How are they different?

Services usually involve singing, prayer, Bible readings, and a sermon.

Most Christian services, also called Mass, include the ceremony of Holy **Communion** (or the Eucharist). In the Bible, Jesus gathered his followers together for a meal, known as the Last Supper. Jesus told them that his death was necessary because it would make a new bond between God and people. Jesus took bread and wine, blessed them, and shared them with his followers.

In the Communion ceremony, Christians eat a special piece of bread and, in some churches, drink a sip of wine or grape juice. In many Christian churches, children make their first Holy Communion when they are about seven years old.

The Holy Communion ceremony is a reminder to Christians that Jesus died for their sins. The lines from the Bible read before receiving Communion include the phrase: "Do this in remembrance of me."

This painting from 1567 by Spanish painter Juan Fernández Navarrete shows a Jewish preacher named John the Baptist baptizing Jesus Christ.

Baptism is also an important ritual for Christians. It involves the spiritual cleansing of sins and acceptance into God's church. During baptism, a person may be sprinkled with water or immersed completely underwater. People of any age may be baptized, though in many Christian churches, people are baptized as infants.

## WORD WISE

COMMUNION IS AN ACT OF SHARING. IN CHRISTIANITY, THE COMMUNION CEREMONY IS SHARED BY THE CHRISTIAN COMMUNITY OR CHURCH CONGREGATION. THE WORD "EUCHARIST" COMES FROM THE GREEK WORD FOR "THANKSGIVING."

# The Christian Bible

The sacred book of Christianity—the Bible—is made up of two main parts: the Old Testament and the New Testament. The Bible was written by many different authors over many hundreds of years. The Old Testament describes how God made a covenant, or agreement, with the people of Israel and chose them to be a special people. The Old Testament also contains the Ten Commandments, laws which say there is one God and describe how to treat others. For example, they forbid stealing, killing, and lying.

After Jesus's death, Christians created the New Testament to spread the message of Jesus. Four books, called the Gospels, tell about Jesus's life and teachings. The Acts of the Apostles tell about the early history of the church and its messengers, or apostles, after Jesus's death. The Epistles are letters of advice and instruction. The last book of the Bible, the Book of Revelation describes the end of the world and ends with the Second Coming of Christ.

The Bible was the first book published using a system of moveable type invented by Johannes Gutenberg around 1455. It helped spread Christianity around the world.

## compare**and**contrast

The Old Testament was based on the main religious text of Judaism, the Hebrew Bible. Can you think of other similarities between Christianity and Judaism? How are they different?

During Mass, a priest or minister reads aloud from the Bible.

# The Life of Jesus

According to the Bible, a woman named Mary gave birth to Jesus in about 6 BCE in Bethlehem, a city in the Middle Eastern region of Palestine. Mary and her husband, Joseph, were Jews from Nazareth, and that is where Jesus grew up. Christians believe that Jesus was the Messiah—a savior sent to save people from sin. The word "Christ" comes from Khristos, the Greek word for Messiah.

The story of the birth of Jesus Christ is called the Nativity. This word comes from the Latin word for "to be born."

Although some stories differ, most sources agree that Jesus spent a part of his life in Nazareth. Some say he was born there, while others say he moved there later in life. Today, Nazareth is part of Isreal.

Little is known of Jesus's youth. There is a story that tells of Jesus, even at a young age, showing interest in religion. It says he spoke with Jewish leaders about faith. Jesus's father on Earth was a carpenter, and many people believe Jesus also became a carpenter.

## Consider This

Scholars have found historical records of Jesus's life, but very little is known about his childhood. Why are historical records important when discussing the lives of people from history?

When he was about thirty years old, Jesus began preaching. He gathered a group of twelve followers, called the Apostles, who helped him spread his message. Many of Jesus's teachings grew out of Judaism. He taught people to honor God and live peaceful, moral lives so they could enter Heaven. He often taught by using parables to explain his message.

Jesus attracted many followers, but not everyone liked his teachings. Jesus welcomed all types of people, even those whom Jewish religious leaders considered to be sinners. Some religious leaders thought that Jesus's teaching was wrong and that it was leading people astray. Others feared that he might start a political uprising, and that this would lead to great trouble. The leaders decided to have Jesus put to death. Jesus was crucified, or nailed to a cross, and died. However, the New Testament says that Jesus resurrected (came back to life) and joined God in heaven.

The Last Supper, which was the first Holy Communion, is a commonly painted scene in Christianity. It shows Jesus and the Apostles eating together shortly before his death.

## compare and contrast

Can you think of any other historical figures who were known to be kind and peaceful? What makes their stories the same as or different from Jesus's story?

Christians believe Jesus died for their sins. The Christian symbol of the cross is meant to symbolize this.

15

# Spreading the Word of Jesus

Jesus's followers grew and continued to practice religion the same way as Jews, except they believed Jesus was a savior sent from God. To help spread Jesus's teachings, some early Christians wrote about him. Writings by four men—Matthew, Mark, Luke, and John—tell of Jesus's life and teachings. These writings now make up the Gospels of the New Testament.

The word "gospel" originally meant the teachings of Jesus Christ, but the term is used for the first four books of the New Testament.

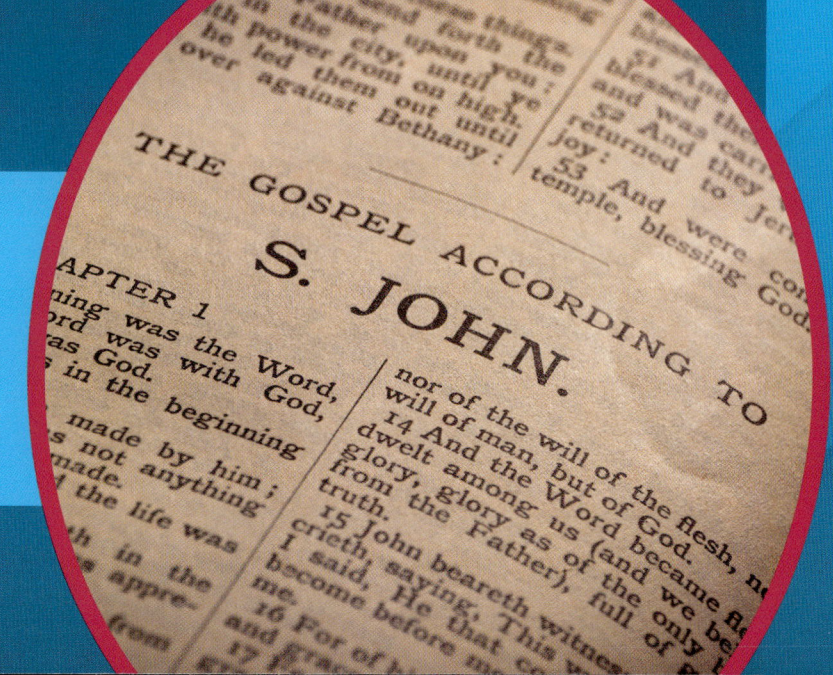

Paul the Apostle was the first Christian missionary to spread Jesus's teachings outside the Jewish community. The main biblical source about his life and teachings can be found in the Acts of the Apostles, part of the New Testament.

Some of Jesus's followers became **missionaries** and moved to other lands. The most important missionary was a man named Paul. Jesus and his earliest followers preached only to the Jewish community, but Paul spread Jesus's teachings to those who were not Jewish.

As the message of Jesus's teaching spread, Christianity was born. In the early days of Christianity, life was difficult and even dangerous for Christians. The government of the Roman Empire, which controlled the region, did not approve of Christianity.

## WORD WISE

A MISSIONARY IS SOMEONE SENT TO SPREAD A RELIGIOUS FAITH AMONG NONBELIEVERS. THEY ARE ALSO CALLED UPON TO DO CHARITABLE WORK.

About 300 years after the resurrection of Christ, Christianity became the official religion of the Roman Empire. A Roman emperor converted to Christianity in 312 CE, which helped create acceptance of Christianity.

Christianity continued to grow during the Middle Ages, a period from about the year 500 CE to about 1500 CE. The leaders of the Christian church became powerful and wealthy, and the church grew to become the most powerful cultural force in Europe.

As Christianity grew, it could not remain unified. In 1054 CE the Eastern church at Constantinople separated from the Western church in Rome because of differences in beliefs and practices. This split created the Roman Catholic Church and the Eastern Orthodox churches.

The Roman emperor Constantine became a Christian in 312 CE. This painting from 1524 shows what his baptism may have looked like.

## compareandcontrast

How are nonreligious leaders (such as a king or president) different from or the same as religious leaders?

The Crusades were a series of wars waged for the purpose of spreading Christianity as far as possible. Many of the battles took place in the Holy Land, which is today Isreal and Palestine.

19

# Branches and Denominations

The Roman Catholic church was very powerful In the early 1500s. Almost everyone in western and central Europe was Roman Catholic. A German priest named Martin Luther began to question certain religious practices of Catholicism. He did not agree with the amount of power and wealth held by the church. Luther also disagreed with many of the rituals used in the church.

Martin Luther's teachings caused a push to change some Catholic practices. This movement is known as the Reformation.

20

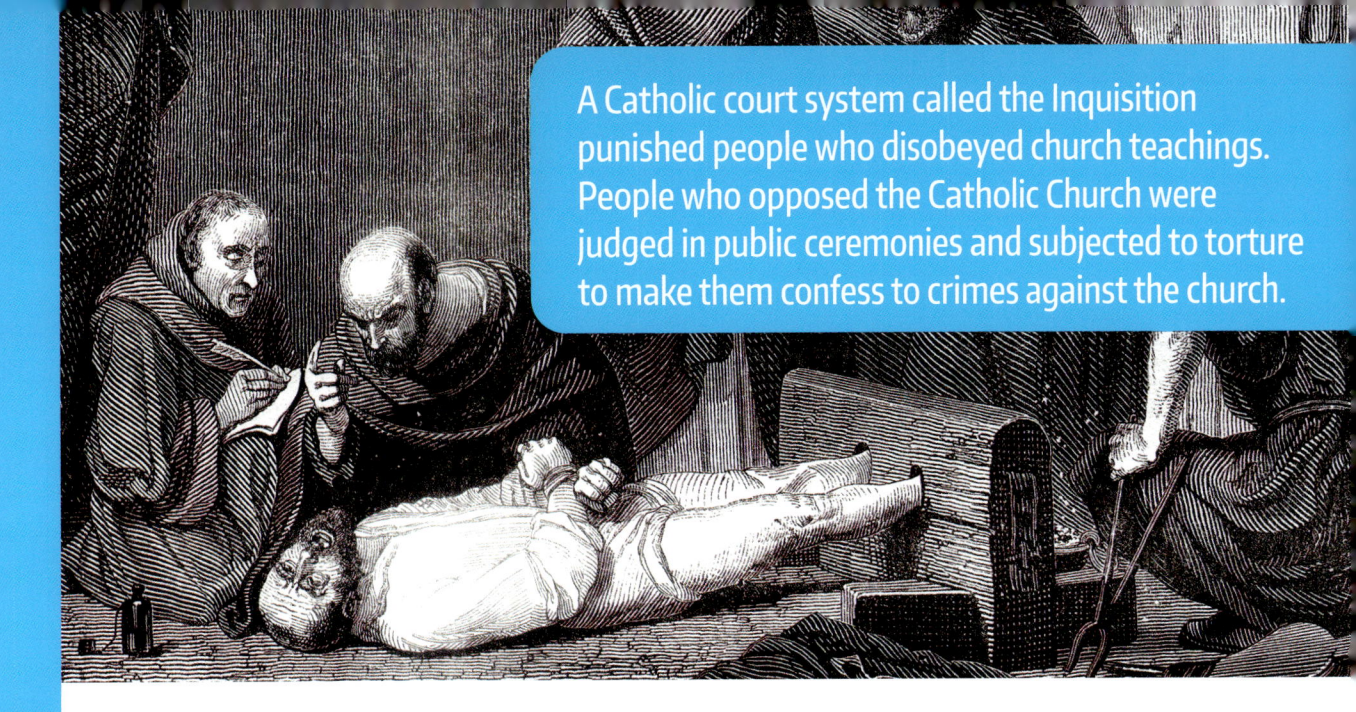

A Catholic court system called the Inquisition punished people who disobeyed church teachings. People who opposed the Catholic Church were judged in public ceremonies and subjected to torture to make them confess to crimes against the church.

Luther's criticism helped bring about the religious revolution known as the Reformation. As a result of the Reformation, the first Protestant churches were founded. The Roman Catholic Church tried to stop the spread of Protestantism with its own movement, the Counter-Reformation. Members of a religious order known as the Jesuits spread Roman Catholicism through their teaching and missionary work.

## Consider This

There have been other groups in history that were treated poorly or even punished for splitting off from a main group or way of thinking. Does this still happen to day? If so, how can people change that?

Europe was mostly divided into Protestant and Catholic regions by the mid-1600s. Most of these divisions have remained in place. In the 1600s the settlers of the British colonies brought Protestantism to North America. With more than 500 million followers today, Protestantism is the second largest branch of Christianity. It is divided into many different **denominations** including the Lutheran, Baptist, Methodist, and Quaker churches.

During the colonial era, Quakers sought greater religious freedom in North America.

Despite the many different branches of Christianity, many Christians choose to go to nondenominational churches. There, all Christians can worship without restrictions.

Although many Protestant churches have different beliefs, all Protestants reject Roman Catholicism and the power of its leader, the pope. They base their beliefs on the Christian Bible. Most believe that getting to heaven requires only faith in God, not any specific actions. They believe that all Protestants, not just priests, can spread the word of God to others.

## WORD WISE

THE WORD DENOMINATION REFERS TO A RELIGIOUS GROUP THAT HAS SLIGHTLY DIFFERENT BELIEFS FROM OTHER GROUPS OF THE SAME RELIGION.

# Celebrations

Christmas, Epiphany, and Easter are three of the most important days of the year for Christians. Christmas celebrates the birth of Jesus. The day and year of his birth are not certain. Roman Catholics and Protestants celebrate Christmas on December 25, and the Eastern Orthodox church celebrates on January 6. Many traditions from around the world are tied to this festive holiday, such as decorating a Christmas tree and exchanging gifts.

Christmas traditions include decorating Christmas trees, exchanging gifts, and charitable activities.

Epiphany celebrations may include parades and dancing.

Another important holiday is Epiphany. The word "epiphany" means "appearance." In the Eastern churches, Epiphany mainly celebrates Jesus's baptism. In the Western church, Christians celebrate Epiphany as the day that the three Wise Men, or Magi, visited the baby Jesus with gifts. For this reason, Epiphany is sometimes called Three Kings Day. Twelfth Night, the evening before Epiphany, is celebrated across Europe.

## Consider This

Many families celebrate Christmas in ways that reflect their cultural roots. Why do you think people celebrate Christmas in different ways? What are some traditions your family celebrate?

The holiest day of the year for Christians is Easter. It celebrates their belief in the resurrection of Jesus Christ. A celebration of new life, Easter occurs in the spring.

In many churches, Easter follows a period of prayer and fasting called Lent. Lent is observed in memory of the forty days Jesus is said to have fasted in the desert. In Roman Catholic and Protestant churches, Lent begins with Ash Wednesday. This day gets its name from the practice of putting ashes on the foreheads of the faithful as a symbol of the season. During Lent, many Christians fast, or go without regular meals, on certain days. Some Christians "fast" during Lent by giving up something that they enjoy, such as a favorite food or a fun activity.

Easter is proceeded by a 40-day period of time called Lent. This is a time for Christians to grow closer to God by praying, fasting, and giving to charity.

Dyeing eggs bright colors and finding baskets full of goodies left by the Easter Bunny is meant to be a celebration of new life.

The week before Easter is known as Holy Week. During this week, Christians remember the events leading up to Jesus's death. The Friday before Easter is known as Good Friday. It is the day on which Jesus was crucified.

## Consider This

Why do you think the day that Jesus was crucified is called "Good" Friday?

# Modern Christianity

Even today, Christian missionaries continue to spread the word of God throughout the world. Christian churches in Africa and Latin America have become important centers of Christianity. In 2013 a priest from Argentina was named pope of the Roman Catholic Church. The pope is the leader of the church throughout the world. Pope Francis is known for his efforts to **revitalize** the Roman Catholic Church and make it more welcoming.

The pope is the leader of the Roman Catholic Church. As of 2025, the Catholic Church has had 266 popes.

The largest Christian churches are sometimes called "megachurches." They can hold tens of thousands of churchgoers at one time!

Today Christianity is the most popular religion in the United States. About 70 percent of the U.S. population is some denomination of Christian. Some Christian churches have large congregations, with memberships numbering in the thousands. Many Christian churches use the internet and television to spread their messages, especially to young worshippers.

## WORD WISE
TO REVITALIZE MEANS TO BRING NEW LIFE TO SOMETHING.

# Glossary

**carpenter** A worker who builds or repairs wooden structures.

**empire** A large territory or a number of territories or peoples under one ruler with total authority.

**Gospel** One of the first four New Testament books telling of the life, death, and resurrection of Jesus Christ.

**humble** Modest; not proud or bold.

**Jesuits** An all-male religious order within the Roman Catholic Church, founded in 1534.

**Middle East** The region around the southern and eastern shores of the Mediterranean Sea.

**minister** A leader of a group of worshippers, especially within a Protestant church.

**moral** Guided by right behavior.

**opposition** Disagreement with someone or something.

**parable** A short simple story illustrating a moral or spiritual truth.

**priest** A religious leader of the Roman Catholic Church.

**region** An area.

**resurrected** Raised from the dead; brought back to life.

**savior** A person that saves others from danger or destruction.

**sermon** A talk that teaches a lesson and is given by a priest or a minister.

**unified** Grouped together as a whole.

**uprising** An act or instance of fighting against authority.

# For More Information

## Books

Bolti, Mary. *Christian Festivals and Tradtitions*. Mankato, MN: Capstone, 2025.

Kennedy, Jared. *The Story of Martin Luther: The Monk Who Changed the World*. Wheaton, IL: Crossawy, 2024.

## Websites

**Christianity Facts for Kids**
*kids.kiddle.co/Christianity*
Learn more about Christianity at this detailed website.

**What Is Christianity?**
*www.bbc.co.uk/bitesize/articles/zvfnkmn*
Read more about the world's most popular religion and see a short video explaining what it is.

# Index